Hit The Inbox

Hit The Inbox

HOW TO AVOID THE SPAM FOLDER AND GROW YOUR BUSINESS WITH EMAIL MARKETING

Scott A. Hartley

MasterPlan4Success

Published by MasterPlan4Success.

Printed in the United States of America.

ISBN: 979-8-9874908-0-8 (paperback)
ISBN: 979-8-9874908-1-5 (eBook)

Acknowledgements
Cover design: Lộc Nguyễn
Copy editor: Susan Carey

Disclaimer
Although the publisher and the author have made every effort to ensure that the information in this book was correct at press time and while this publication is designed to provide accurate information in regard to the subject matter covered, the publisher and the author assume no responsibility for errors, inaccuracies, omissions, or any other inconsistencies herein and hereby disclaim any liability to any party for any loss, damage, or disruption caused by errors or omissions, whether such errors or omissions result from negligence, accident, or any other cause.

This publication is meant as a source of valuable information for the reader; however, it is not meant as a substitute for direct expert assistance. If such level of assistance is required, the services of a competent professional should be sought.

Hit The Inbox is a trademark of MasterPlan4Success.

All trademarks and copyrighted items mentioned throughout this book are the property of their respective owners.

Reviews

"*Hit The Inbox* is a super practical resource that unpacks a complicated, technical topic. Many people understand the value of needing email marketing, but don't take the time to ensure that investment is maximized. I 100% recommend checking this out. It's well worth the investment!"

- Evan Cox, Evan Cox Consulting

"Scott's book is no-nonsense, easy to read, and has many ah-ha strategies that will help you get better results with your email marketing—highly recommended."

- Dave Dee, Author of *Sales Stampede*

"Scott has a way of simplifying the (seemingly) complicated subject of email deliverability. Not only does he tell you the truth about what it takes to 'hit the inbox,' but he also shares actionable steps that you can take to improve your results. And he's right, if you follow his recommendations, you will definitely have an unfair advantage over your competition."

- Misty Kortes, Your Marketing Coach

"While other books have spines, this book has balls. A quick and powerful, game-changing read. I used to think people didn't reply because my copy sucked, but after reading *Hit The Inbox,* I learned my emails weren't getting to the inbox. People can't respond to an email that they don't see. Now instead of getting the occasional reply, I'm now getting multiple replies in a single day."

- Dan Shea, Author of *Cold2Sold*

"In a read that took me significantly shorter than sitting through a series of webinars on the same subject, Scott Hartley concisely and credibly delivers the critical information you need to know about getting your emails into inboxes instead of spam or junk folders.

Moreover, the methods he describes are often overlooked by seasoned professionals and can have a much greater impact than many of the typical tactics used in the industry."

- Scott Ruesch, Ruesch Consulting

Contents

A Personal Letter From Scott Hartley

Since you picked up a copy of this book, you likely use email marketing to reach your prospects and customers.

You probably also either:

1. **Know you have problems** with people seeing your emails, causing you to lose sales, and want to fix them ASAP ... or
2. **Want to proactively prevent issues** and generate as much interest and revenue as possible from your email list.

If this is you, you're in the right place.

I've written this book because I want to help you capitalize on the time, effort, and investment you're putting into your email marketing.

Isn't email marketing dead?

Some people proclaim email marketing is dead.

I disagree.

I know businesses just like yours who rake in hundreds of thousands, even millions, of dollars every year using email as <u>one</u> of their marketing media. *(Never rely on any one means to reach your ideal customer - including email. Explaining this further is a topic for another time.)*

Yes, getting emails delivered is more challenging.

Yes, people's inboxes are flooded with more emails.

Yes, it takes work to leverage the power of email to reach your audience.

But email marketing is **NOT** dead - not even close.

I know I'm preaching to the choir because you're here reading this book. I simply want to make sure you're not led astray by uninformed or biased "gurus" who would say otherwise.

Your most valuable asset

Building **your own list** of prospects and customers is one of your business' most valuable assets.

Building **a relationship** with your list *exponentially* increases its value.

One way to do that is through email communication - *done the right way.*

When you apply the secrets I reveal in the chapters ahead, you'll begin to discover this truth for yourself.

You'll be celebrating as you steadily see more people reading your emails and clicking your calls to action - whether that's opting in for a lead magnet, scheduling an appointment, purchasing your product or service, or something else.

Your "unfair" advantage

The bad news is Google, Microsoft, Yahoo, and every other mailbox provider makes it increasingly difficult to get your emails delivered and seen.

The good news is your competitors (and the majority of small business owners in general) have **no interest** in discovering the secrets you're reading here - let alone actually applying them.

Their ignorance and apathy gives you an "unfair" advantage - making *your* email marketing easier and more profitable.

In the summer of 2022, I randomly analyzed the technical configurations - the settings required for getting emails delivered - of 200 small businesses who were using a bulk email marketing platform.

92% of them had *at least one* - and in most cases two - critical issues that would cause problems getting their emails seen by their recipients.

I provided the business owners screenshots showing the errors and explained how they dramatically reduced the effectiveness of their email marketing.

I offered them a no-cost, no-obligation comprehensive audit of their email marketing - examining all the things you'll learn about in this book.

The audit would give them their real-time email health score and reveal any other potential problems negatively impacting their email outreach. It would identify the steps they needed to take to fix any problems.

Not a single one of them responded.

Sadly, they inflict more damage on their email reputation with every email blast they send.

But that's good news for you.

When you finish reading this book - and take action on what you learn, you'll be one of the few business owners whose emails take your business - and revenue - to the next level.

Helping you win the game,

Scott A. Hartley

Visit **HitTheInboxBook.com** to request your Hit The Inbox™ audit and explore other valuable resources.

Can You Handle The Truth About Email?

Before I dive into revealing the four secrets to landing your emails in your recipients' inboxes, I need to make sure you understand - and accept - five basic truths about email.

Everything I present later will make more sense with these in mind.

Only two things in life are certain;
Getting your email delivered isn't one of them.

Benjamin Franklin rightly said, "In this world, nothing is certain except death and taxes."

While technology, for the most part, is very reliable, **email is not a guaranteed service**.

Several reasons exist why someone might not receive your email:

1. The address is invalid.
2. A problem occurred with the email account or mail server.
3. Your message was rejected as spam.

Simply put, mailbox providers are under <u>no obligation</u> to accept or deliver what you want to send.

The Gmail Promotions tab isn't seriously hurting you.

I can count on one hand the number of conversations I've had where the other person *didn't* bring up their emails landing in Gmail's Promotions tab.

By the way many email marketers talk, you'd think every last one of them was losing millions of dollars a year because of this.

While it's true that the Promotions tab has an overall lower open rate, it's only 3% less than the Primary tab.[1]

And...

- Only 1 in 5 Gmail users has the Promotions tab enabled.[2]
- 45% of users with the Promotions tab enabled check it daily.[3]

And when you do the math looking at the <u>whole</u> picture, the numbers tell a different story.

> *"Only 1 in 5 Gmail users have the Promotions tab enabled, and 22% of the addresses on a typical email list are Gmail users. That means that only about 5% of the normal ... user's contacts have the Promotions tab enabled.* **Therefore, on average, Promotional placement would only lower your open rate <u>by about one-half a percentage point</u>,** *at the most."* (emphasis added)[4]

It's not worth your time and energy agonizing over your emails showing up in Promotions.

And whatever you do, don't try shady tricks to avoid the Promotions tab that some email marketers suggest. Google severely punishes anyone who tries to game their system.

Ironically, I recently received an email from a consultant offering his $10,000 "stay out of the promo tab" solution.

Guess where his email landed?

In my promo tab!

If you adopt the recommendations I outline in the chapters ahead, you won't have to scheme your way to getting your emails landing in the inbox.

Unwanted messages pollute the Internet.

85% of the more than 306 billion emails sent daily are spam.[5, 6]

You see this every day when you open the email app on your phone or computer.

Dozens of unwanted messages clutter both your inbox and spam/junk folders multiple times throughout the day. It's practically a full-time job to constantly remove them!

Spam emails generally come from three sources.

1. Legitimate businesses and salespeople.

> Somehow your email address got added to their list, but you've never given them permission to email you.

> Many are either unaware of the laws governing email communication, or they simply choose to ignore them.

> This group uses the spray-and-pray method of email marketing because it's cheap and easy.

> They hope that by sending enough emails to enough people, it

will generate more phone calls and sales with less work than other forms of marketing.

2. Individuals looking to make a quick buck.

> This group of spammers looks to make boatloads of money with as little effort as possible.
>
> They scrape the Internet for or buy lists of email addresses, then blast out their offers promoting work-from-home jobs, miracle potions, cryptocurrency investment opportunities, and other questionable goods and services.

3. Hackers and criminals.

> Emails from these spammers can cost you thousands of dollars and hours of time.
>
> Their messages often mimic the look of emails sent by well-known companies, like Fed-Ex, UPS, and Chase Bank.
>
> Containing malicious links, these emails can silently install malware on your computer to monitor every site you visit and letter you type.
>
> Or you may be taken to a fictitious website where you're directed to enter in usernames, passwords, and other personal or financial information.
>
> You'll soon discover they've gained access to your bank accounts, credit cards, email accounts, and social media profiles.

You must follow their rules.

To help keep their users safe and to safeguard their networks, the big three mailbox providers - Microsoft, Google, and Yahoo - each enforce their own set of rules that determines whether your email is accepted or rejected.

And if it's accepted, where it will be placed.

But because bad people (spammers) abuse rules designed to protect us and make our lives more convenient with technology, none of the mailbox providers reveal the algorithms they use to make their decisions.

They only share a select few, vague details that can help you increase your chances of getting your emails accepted.

Everything else boils down to testing.

There's no magic bullet.

No checklist exists that, when you check all the boxes, guarantees your email will make it to the inbox or get a high open rate.

Only by testing different things - and following the guidelines in this book - will you be able to see what works for your particular list.

There's an **art _and_ science** behind getting your emails to Hit The Inbox™ so they get opened and acted upon.

Now that you understand the truths about email, you're ready to discover Secret #1.

KEY TAKEAWAYS

1. Email is not a guaranteed service.

2. Don't agonize over your emails landing in the Google Promotions tab. It's not as detrimental as you may think.

3. Your marketing emails compete with billions of spam emails.

4. Mailbox providers - Google, Microsoft, and Yahoo - make the rules by which you must abide to get your emails delivered.

5. There's an **art _and_ science** behind getting your emails to Hit The Inbox™. Only by testing will you determine what works for your list and your business.

Secret #1: Engagement Matters Most

The most effective action you can take to land more of your emails in your recipients' inboxes is to **manage your engagement**.

This can single-handedly boost your email reputation with the big 3 mailbox providers - Google, Microsoft, and Yahoo.

Being in their good graces sometimes gives you a little more latitude in the other areas we'll discuss later, especially Secret #3.

Levels Of Engagement

Engagement must be monitored and managed on three levels.

1. Your **entire list** - how the majority of your contacts interact with your emails
2. **All contacts using a particular mailbox provider** - how a large number of your contacts using Google or Microsoft as their mailbox provider, for example, interact with your emails
3. The **individual contact** - how each person interacts with your emails

Where your emails end up heavily depends on what the <u>majority</u> of your list does with your messages.

If most of your contacts never open your emails, it's very likely your future emails will soon end up in junk or spam - <u>even for the handful of contacts who *do* engage</u> with every email you send.

Timeframes Of Engagement

Google, Microsoft, and Yahoo each use different timeframes to determine a person's engagement with your emails.

Microsoft defines engagement as what someone has done with your email in the last **14 days**. Because of this and other reasons, you'll find getting your emails delivered to people who use Microsoft's email services (Hotmail.com, Live.com, Outlook.com, and Microsoft 365) more difficult.

Yahoo offers a more relaxed view of engagement. They look at the last **30 to 60 days**.

Google uses a **30 to 90 day window** <u>and</u> also considers how often you're emailing, how many people you're emailing to on their platform, and what your overall email reputation is.

I recommend you use 90 days to determine your list's engagement as you begin to improve your email health using the strategies in this book.

You will eventually want to reduce that down to 30 days, especially if most of your contacts use Microsoft as their mailbox provider, and no more than 60 days.

How To Boost Engagement

Now that you understand the levels and timeframes the big 3 mailbox providers use to assess engagement, you're wondering what specific steps you can take to manage and boost it.

Here are five actions to take.

Tell Subscribers What To Do

Most of your contacts will join your list through a form on your website. Maybe they request a lead magnet, sign up for a webinar, or enroll in a course.

On the **thank you page** of every opt-in and order form, provide your subscriber with **clear next steps** on how to find your email and what to do with it.

You can also provide the same instructions in your first email after someone opts in or purchases.

You'll understand why this is so important on page 14.

Here are a couple examples you can model from The Betty Rocker website.[7, 8]

YOU'RE ALMOST DONE!

1
Check your email.
If you can't find it in your inbox, **check your spam/junk or promotions folder, and move it to your Inbox.** Make sure you used your BEST email address (and didn't - oops - mis-type!)

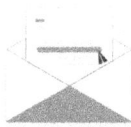

2
Click the confirmation link.

3
Enjoy all the great content I'm sending your way!

THANK **YOU!**

I've just emailed you your **Berry Green Protein Recipe Guide!**
I can't wait to hear what you make!

If you don't see your guide in your inbox, be sure to check your other email folders or spam, in case it got rerouted. Drag the email into your inbox and mark me as a safe sender, or add my to your contacts so you don't miss my emails!

Set Proper Expectations

Whenever somebody opts in to your list, set expectations for how you're going to communicate with them.

First, let them know **how often** you will be emailing them.

You should do this for both short-term sequences, such as where you'll be sending reminder emails for an upcoming webinar, and long-term series, like a nurture campaign.

Whatever your cadence, be clear about it. This avoids any surprises when your emails appear in their inbox.

Second, **remind them** how they got on your list.

Never assume a person will remember why they opted in for your emails. They may have forgotten they requested your lead magnet or attended your webinar.

You can place copy in the footer of your emails to jog their memory. The more specific you can be, the better.

Finally, **sell them on the value** you'll be providing through your upcoming email content.

Use curiosity bullets to tease what you'll be sharing in future emails.[9]

Build up the excitement that makes them look forward to receiving communication from you.

Make It Easy To Unsubscribe

Ever experience the feelings of sadness, disappointment, and loss when you see that someone unsubscribed from your list?

It hurts.

After all, you're doing your best to help them by offering your advice and products or services.

Some email marketers go to great lengths to avoid these painful feelings and make unsubscribing from their list nearly impossible.

But if you want to boost your engagement, you need to let people who no longer want to hear from you remove themselves from your list easily.

Attempts to keep them from unsubscribing only work against you …

Because they'll mark your email as spam.

Which raises red flags with Google, Microsoft, and Yahoo *and* your email marketing software.

Frequency

Let's do some math.

You send Johnny, a prospective customer on your list, a nurture email once a month, but he doesn't open it.

What is Johnny's engagement score?

It's a big fat zero.

Now if you send Johnny four emails over that same 30 day period, and he opens one of them, his engagement rate is 25 percent.

If he opens two, it's 50 percent.

You can multiply this out for the total number of people on your list. The math works the same.

See how sending more frequent emails gives you more opportunities to bump up your engagement score?

A Common Objection

You're likely saying under your breath, *"Scott, if I email my list more than once a month, bad things will happen. They'll get tired of hearing from me. People will unsubscribe. I'll get hateful replies. It's not worth it."*

Let me ask you a couple questions.

How often do you talk to your significant other or your best friend?

More than once a month, right?

Do they ever get tired of hearing from you, respond with hateful comments, or tell you to never speak to them again?

Of course they don't. It's ludicrous to even think.

Why?

They like you - that's a given.

But each conversation you have, you're bringing something of value that's interesting to them.

When you approach communicating with your list the same way, **sending more emails deepens your relationship with each person.**

They look forward to hearing what you have to share - as long as you're not constantly blasting them with "buy my stuff" messages.

That's not to say some people won't remove themselves from your list or send you nasty replies.

It's ok if those few do. Don't take it personally (I know, easier said than done!).

They weren't your ideal customer and probably would never have bought from you.

Consistency

Once you've decided how often you'll communicate with your list, you need to stick to it.

Infrequent and inconsistent communication often results in a spike of unsubscribes and spam complaints.

People forget that they opted in to your list.

Or they're no longer interested in hearing from you because the know, like, and trust factor they once had with you diminished due to the extended silence.

Also **Google, Microsoft, and Yahoo reward consistency**.

Spammers notoriously blast emails in spurts in their efforts to try to game the system.

When you inconsistently send emails, skipping weeks or months at a time, your behavior begins to look like that of spammers.

And your reputation takes a hit.

STOP!
Don't send more emails until you read this!

You **_do_** need to send more emails more frequently and more consistently.

But unless you understand that your list is made up of assets and liabilities - and what to do about them - you risk **severely damaging** your reputation with Google, Microsoft, and Yahoo, and causing your emails to end up in junk or spam.

Assets

Assets are the contacts who help put you in good standing with the mailbox providers.

Your goal is to have the majority of your list filled with assets.

Their behaviors increase your engagement score. Here's a list of what they consistently do:

- Open most or all of your emails
- Click on links in your emails
- Reply to your emails
- Forward your emails to others
- Whitelist your email address
- Move your emails to their inbox folder
- File your emails into a specific folder

These people are the ones you *should* continue communicating with frequently and consistently.

Liabilities

On the other hand, liabilities are the contacts dragging down your email reputation with the mailbox providers.

Their behaviors negatively impact your engagement score, such as:

- Deleting your emails without opening them
- Moving your emails to junk or spam
- Marking your emails as spam

You should immediately stop emailing these people.

Yahoo warns us that "sending email to users who are not reading them … will harm your delivery metrics and reputation."[10]

Eventually you've got to cut your losses and say, *Hey, this person is not interested at this point in time. It doesn't mean that they won't be interested again in the future, but right now they're not interested in what I have to offer, so let's stop sending them emails.*

When you remove the liabilities from your list, your assets will begin to see more of your emails in their inbox.

Let's look at some numbers again to see how this works.

Let's say on your list of 1,000 contacts, 500 of those people use Gmail as their provider.

If Gmail subscriber engagement is low, meaning that maybe 50 of your 500 contacts are engaging, then Gmail will treat the entire 500 the same way.

Because 450 people are not opening up your email for whatever reason, Gmail is going to put you into the Promotions tab or into the Updates tab, and do the same with the 50 who are actually engaging.

What impacts the 450 is also impacting the 50.

When you get those liabilities, the unengaged contacts, off your list and only send to the 50, that works in your favor.

Segmentation

Is it possible to make 760% more revenue from an email campaign?

Research performed by the Data & Marketing Association says it is when you send segmented email campaigns instead of a one-size-fits all.[11]

Segmentation is sending emails to **smaller groups of subscribers based on certain criteria** with messages that appeal to that particular audience.

A Real World Example

Let's walk through a recent campaign for a winery that promoted a new release - Cabernet Merlot.

The first step was to focus on the list of assets - people who have purchased red wine in the last 90 days.

We knew that they like red wine.

We knew that they are active buyers and that they've opened up emails in the last 90 days.

That segmentation led to an open rate of 72 percent and a click-through rate of 21 percent, which resulted in higher sales.

To test the theory, we looked at the results using a different segmentation.

The list of liabilities included people who have never bought red wine and who have not opened up an email in 180 or more days.

The open rate was only 3 percent and the click-through rate was less than 1 percent.

As you can see, when we combine segmentation with sending only to engaged contacts, more people open the email and more people buy.

Ways To Segment Your List

The makeup of your list will be different from that of another business. So how you segment your list will also be different.

Here are some ways you can consider slicing up your list for precise email communication:

- Geography

- Age/Birthday

- Gender

- Income

- Industry

- Past Purchases

- Interests

- Frequency Of Purchase

- Amount Of Purchase

- Type Of Purchase

- Customer Lifetime Value

- Engagement Level

- People Who Refer

- Event/Webinar Attendance

- New Subscribers

- By Lead Magnet

- Abandoned Shopping Cart

Is your email list made up of mostly assets or liabilities?

Are you damaging your email reputation with every email you send?

Find out for sure by requesting your Hit The Inbox™ audit at **HitTheInboxBook.com**. Use promo code **BOOK20** to receive $20 off.

KEY TAKEAWAYS

1. Managing your engagement is your most effective tool to get more of your emails delivered and seen.

2. What the majority of your recipients do with your emails plays a major role in how mailbox providers handle your messages.

3. Each mailbox provider uses different timeframes to measure engagement - from 14 days to 90 days.

4. Design your thank-you pages to give clear steps on what people should do with your emails.

5. Emailing your list frequently (at least weekly) and consistently provides your audience more opportunities to engage.

6. Contacts on your email list are either assets or liabilities. Assets increase your engagement score; liabilities decrease it.

7. Prune your list as soon as possible of all liabilities.

8. Sending targeted emails to segments of your list will always outperform an email blast to your entire audience.

Secret #2:
Authentication Makes
You Legit

My grandma lived a block away from my house when I was growing up. So I'd often walk down the street and spend time with her.

One afternoon, when I was about eleven or twelve years old, she needed something from the grocery store.

We hopped into her white Chevrolet Caprice Classic (that had a red cloth interior and an 8-track player!) and headed to the west side of our small town.

As we neared the top of the overpass, the sun blinded my grandma so badly that she couldn't see to continue driving.

From the passenger seat, I grabbed the steering wheel with one hand and guided the car safely down the opposite side, where she was able to resume driving.

Although I didn't have a driver's license and I wasn't of legal age, I still drove on a public roadway - even if it was for only a quarter of a mile.

Luckily, we didn't get pulled over or have an accident. Otherwise, my grandma and I could have faced serious consequences.

What does this story have to do with email marketing?, you ask.

Anyone - including you - can send emails to anyone in the world anytime you like.

You can even do so without having the proper authentication configured on your sending domain.[12]

And for a while, you might not experience any issues.

But at some point, mailbox providers - like Google, Microsoft, or Yahoo - and spam filters - like Proofpoint and Barracuda, commonly used in many B2B organizations - will "pull you over" like a traffic cop and perform a deeper inspection on one of your emails.

And that's where being legit by having authentication set up becomes critically important.

Why Providers Require Authentication

The Internet can be a lot like the Wild West, filled with people doing what they want, when they want, with little regard for others.

Sadly, thousands of people get bilked out of millions of dollars every year by scammers and other criminals.

These unscrupulous characters often use email to perpetrate their deceptive acts.

Mailbox providers use authentication to **protect three parties**:

1. **Your recipients**. To help reduce their risk of receiving scam emails.

2. **You as an email marketer**. To prevent your sending domain from being spoofed and used to send scam emails.

3. **The providers themselves**. To reduce the number of scam emails flooding their servers and to safeguard their business' financial interests.

Why You Need Authentication Configured

First, authentication provides instructions to mailbox providers on **what to do with your email**.

Should they accept or reject it?

Should they trust that it's really been sent from you?

Should they place it in the inbox or junk/spam?

The more proof you can provide them to answer those questions, the better your chances of having your recipients receive and see your emails.

Without authentication, each of the mailbox providers use only their own rules to make assumptions about your email and determine how to handle it.

Second, authentication **reduces your liability risk**.

You are responsible for everything that happens associated with your domain.

You could be held liable if someone gets scammed off an email sent from your domain because you didn't protect it by setting up authentication.

The 3 Authentication Records

Imagine you're cruising down the highway, windows down and your favorite song blaring through your speakers.

You glance in your rearview mirror and see the flashing red and blue lights atop the police car racing to catch up with you.

You pull over, and the police officer walks up to your window.

What three things are you asked to show?

Driver's license, registration, proof of insurance.

You gotta have those three things to legally drive a vehicle on the road, right?

Similarly, you need three records configured on your sending domain's DNS to satisfy the demands of mailbox providers.

DKIM

The first and **most important** authentication record you need to add is known as DKIM, which stands for Domain Keys Identified Mail.

Using our driving analogy, DKIM records function like your driver's license.

By inserting a digital signature into every email, it **proves that you sent the email and are an authorized user of the sending domain**.

DKIM prevents spoofing of your email address.

Spoofing occurs when a spammer or hacker changes the *From:* address of an email to look like it's coming from someone else.

When you have DKIM configured, any emails impersonating your domain will be rejected by mailbox providers.

It's a best practice to create a separate DKIM record for every platform from which you send email.

For example, if you use Microsoft 365 as your primary mailbox provider to send individual emails and also use ActiveCampaign to send mass emails to your list, you need to have two DKIM records - one for Microsoft 365 and one for ActiveCampaign.

SPF

The second authentication record you need to add is known as SPF, which stands for Sender Policy Framework.

This functions like your vehicle registration.

SPF **proves the systems you're using to send emails on your behalf are authorized to do so**.

Here's what a valid SPF record looks like:

```
v=spf1 include:_spf.google.com include:infusionmail.com include:19714098.spf10.hubspotemail.net include:zoho.com ~all
```

Example of a valid SPF record

Your SPF record should contain *include:* statements for all platforms you use to send email. So if you send emails from Google Workspace, Keap, and Hubspot, all three would need to be listed in your SPF record.

When setting up your SPF record, be sure to avoid these common errors:

- Creating more than one SPF record per domain.

- Not including all platforms from which you send emails.

- Having more than 10 DNS lookups.

- Setting too strict a qualifier for how mailbox providers should handle messages that don't match your SPF. (I recommend using ~*all* at the end of your SPF record.)

DMARC

The last authentication record you need to set up is known as DMARC, which stands for Domain-Based Message, Authentication, Reporting and Conformance.

As we continue with our driving analogy, your DMARC record is your proof of insurance.

Its purpose is to tell Google, Microsoft, and Yahoo **what to do with your email** in the event an email you send doesn't pass DKIM or SPF.

Let's suppose you run an eCommerce store using Shopify. You send order confirmations and receipts via email from their platform.

If your SPF record doesn't say that you're sending emails from Shopify, the DMARC record guides Google, Microsoft, and Yahoo what to do with those emails instead of simply rejecting them based on their own rules.

A valid DMARC record looks like this:

```
v=DMARC1; p=none; sp=none; rua=mailto:re-1111446601e@inbound.commerciagents.com; pct=100
```

Example of a valid DMARC record

DMARC also provides you with **regular reports**. These reports tell you every platform and IP address sending emails using your domain, as well as identify the messages that failed DKIM or SPF.

You can use these reports to quickly discover if your domain is being spoofed.

Interpreting DMARC reports requires an advanced understanding of extensible markup language.

I recommend using a third-party DMARC monitoring service to receive and translate the reports into meaningful charts and data.

Some Words Of Warning

Before you rush off to authenticate your domain, consider these important points.

Don't Set Up Authentication Prematurely

Authentication is undoubtedly very important, as you'll learn more in a moment.

But you must **first correct any issues with your engagement and reputation**, as those two factors carry the most weight with mailbox providers.

Until authentication is set up, you're using the reputation of the platforms from which you're sending emails. But there may be problems with your own domain reputation that you can't readily see.

Configuring authentication without the proper due diligence could have very bad consequences.

In one case I'm aware of, a small business owner had a 35% open rate and 5% click rate without having authentication configured.

His open rate tanked to 2% as soon he set up authentication. And it took three months for him to recover.

And of course cost him lots of sales during that time.

But Get It Set Up ASAP

Google, Microsoft, and Yahoo increasingly look at authentication to help reduce the amount of spam flowing through their mail servers.

Microsoft already looks heavily at authentication. Without all three properly configured records, your emails stand a higher probability of landing in the junk folder.

If you notice low open and click rates on any Microsoft-related email address (Microsoft 365, Outlook.com, Live.com, Hotmail.com), this may be one factor.

Google and Yahoo will soon be doing the same.

So make it a priority to correct any engagement and reputation issues so you can set up your authentication.

Make Sure It's Done Right

Although I've attempted to provide a thorough explanation of the various authentication records, it requires a deeper mastery than I can include here.

Setting up authentication requires a bit of technical acumen.

One wrong letter, one wrong dash, one wrong question mark, or using a tilde instead of a dash can create unintended, negative results.

Don't assume that your web guy or IT specialist can configure the records correctly.

I've seen several instances where a computer whiz or web designer botched up an SPF or DMARC record, causing ***all emails*** to get rejected.

Hiring a certified email deliverability consultant is a solid investment - saving you time, money, and headaches.

Do you have all the necessary authentication set up for your domain? Is your authentication configured correctly?

Get the answers by requesting your Hit The Inbox™ audit at **HitTheInboxBook.com/audit.** Use promo code **BOOK20** to receive $20 off.

KEY TAKEAWAYS

1. You need 3 authentication records configured on your sending domain: DKIM, SPF, and DMARC.

2. The DKIM record proves that you sent the email and are an authorized user of the sending domain. It prevents spoofing of your domain.

3. The SPF record proves the systems you're using to send emails on your behalf are authorized to do so.

4. The DMARC record ties everything together. It tells mailbox providers what to do with your email in the event an email you send doesn't pass DKIM or SPF.

5. Before implementing your authentication records, fix engagement and domain reputation issues first. Otherwise, you could have unintended and unexpected ill effects.

6. Authentication records must be created properly. Hire an expert who's set these up before.

Secret #3: Revamp Your Content

You don't just want your emails delivered to the inbox of your recipients.

You want them to take action on your emails - reading your content, requesting your lead magnets, and purchasing your products and services.

The format and content of your emails affect both <u>where</u> your emails land and <u>what</u> people do with them.

Rules vs. Recommendations

What I've shared in all the other secrets of this book are *rules* you need to abide by. Breaking them will eventually cause you serious problems.

But when it comes to what you put in your emails and how you design them, this chapter offers *best practices* and *recommendations* that you should *test* with your specific audience to see what gives you the best results - both with engagement (people opening your emails) and with conversion (sales or opt-ins generated from your emails).

These suggestions originate from helping hundreds of small business owners like yourself, examining millions of emails, and reviewing studies conducted by respected email marketing experts and companies.

As a rule of thumb, you'll want to be **more discerning and stringent with business critical emails** than general communication ones.

With that in mind, let's explore the four primary areas where you should revamp your email content.

Copy

Magazines surround you as you patiently wait in the supermarket checkout line.

Catchy, curiosity-inducing headlines grab your attention - making it almost impossible to avoid snatching up the magazine and flipping to the article to see what it's about.

The subject lines of your emails need to **create the same type of reaction** - forcing people to immediately open your email when they see it appear in their inbox.

However, you cannot use such extreme clickbait-type subject lines if you want your emails to land in the inbox.

Google, Microsoft, and Yahoo **heavily scrutinize** your subject line, your preview text, and your calls-to-action for spammy content. They also examine the individual words and the context of those words in your body copy to determine if it's promotional in nature.

Make It Personal

Even though your marketing emails go to hundreds or thousands of people, you should **write your copy as if you were sending the email to one person**.

What does a personal email look like?

- It's **personalized**. It contains the first name of the recipient somewhere in the copy, usually the greeting or subject line.

- It's **conversational**. You tell stories. You write about something that interests the recipient (segmenting your list allows you to easily achieve this).

- It uses **normal punctuation**. You avoid overuse of exclamation points, question marks, and all caps.

- It's **brief**. Shorter emails get read. Especially since many people check email on a mobile device.

  Longer copy should be placed on your website or in a PDF. Inviting readers to visit your website or take another action to get more details helps with engagement and increases conversions.

Reword Your CTAs

Almost every email marketer's go-to phrase for their call-to-action starts with *Click here.*

- *Click here to schedule a call.*

- *Click here to request your free copy.*

- *Click here for more information.*

This phrase screams "this is a marketing email" to the algorithms.

Take 30 seconds to reword your call-to-action.

- *Visit this page.*

- *Find a time to chat with me.*

- *Learn more about how this works here.*

- *Request your free copy online.*

You'll find that more descriptive, clear calls-to-action will cause more of your readers to do what you ask them.

Context Matters

One simple word or phrase **can make the difference** between your email hitting the inbox or being placed into the Promotions tab or the spam folder.

Now if you happen to include a spam word or phrase in an email, it may have little effect if you're using it in context in your email copy <u>and</u> are abiding by all of the other rules of email marketing.

Several online sites provide commonly known spam trigger words.[13, 14, 15]

You can also paste your email copy into an online tool and have it inspected for potential spam words.[16]

The bottom line is: Your email content needs to be relevant and engaging.

Links

As you discovered in Secret #1, one of the best ways to increase engagement with your emails is by inviting recipients to visit your website, opt in for a lead magnet, or make a purchase.

Links in your emails provide the means for getting your readers where you would like them to go.

Let's explore five guidelines to keep in mind as you insert links into your messages.

Limit The Number Of Links

How many times have you stood in line at a fast food restaurant and the person in front of you stares at the menu for 10 minutes pondering what they want to eat?

Because they're hungry - and after hearing the impatient sighs of the customers waiting behind them - they eventually make up their mind and order.

But that doesn't happen when they're reading your email.

The Psychology Behind This

Your reader quickly decides if your email can be consumed and acted upon immediately or if they should delete it.

If your email gives them multiple actions to take or is filled with links for different things, **they'll do nothing**.

You've heard the adage, "A confused mind always says no."

No, I'm not buying.

No, I'm not watching that video.

No, I'm not taking time to figure out if any of these things interest me.

And if they discard your email, it can hurt your engagement over time.

The Practical Implications

Google, Microsoft, and Yahoo frown on emails containing lots of links, a common characteristic of spam emails.

It doesn't matter if all of them point to the same place or different ones.

Even though your links may point to the same location, email marketing platforms turn each link into a unique one for tracking purposes. So mailbox providers only see different links.

A good rule of thumb is **no more than three total links per email**, no matter where they point.

This includes those in your body copy, images, buttons, social media icons, and even your signature block.

Point Only To Secure Sites

Hackers use unsecure websites to steal people's information. These are the ones without *https:* preceding the web address or that don't have the lock appear next to the web address in your browser's address bar.

Linking to unsecure sites can cause your emails to go straight to spam or contain a warning message emblazoned across the top cautioning the recipient to be careful with the message, which most people will delete out of fear.

Only link to websites that contain *https:* in their web address.

Be Careful Where Your Links Point

When I worked in law enforcement, we maintained a database of **"known associates."**

This repository of drug dealers, violent criminals, sexual predators, and other serious law breakers listed the names of citizens whom they often associated with and where.

Many of the associated individuals didn't have a criminal record or had only committed minor offenses.

But when a known associate was pulled over on a traffic stop or otherwise interacting with the police, the officer would often be more suspicious and thorough in his investigation.

A similar scenario plays out with your emails, especially if you're linking to websites you don't own or control.

If you link to a website that appears on a blocklist, it can affect **where your email gets placed**, often ending up in junk or spam.

Long-term, it **damages your own reputation** simply because you've included that website in one or more of your emails. You're associated with "bad behavior."

Before inserting a link to a third-party website in your email, check to see if the domain or web server appears on any blocklists.[17] If it does, you're wise for not including it.

In Secret #4, we'll discuss in depth the importance of your own domain reputation and how to keep it clean.

Minimize The Use Of Social Media Links

You want people to know all the ways they can interact with you.

This may tempt you to insert links to all your social media channels, like Facebook, LinkedIn, Instagram, YouTube, and TikTok, in your emails.

Before you do, consider why this may not be a good idea.

First, social media websites often **temporarily appear on blocklists**. If one you link to in your email happens to be on there at the time you send it, it can cause your email to get relegated to the junk or spam folder. And it can damage your reputation, as I described in the previous section.

Second, you'll get **better results** from your marketing efforts by consistently driving traffic to your website or a landing page on your domain.

Not only does it help your SEO, but it trains your audience to visit your website.

Third, remember what you learned earlier about the psychology behind limiting the number of links in emails.

Each email's purpose should be to get the reader to take one specific action. Unless you only want them to visit one of your social media channels, including social media links as **additional options can cause indecision**.

A common question I'm asked is, "*Should I embed or link to a YouTube video in my email?*"

My answer is, "*It depends on the purpose of that YouTube video in your email.*"

If your goal is to increase subscribers on your YouTube channel, then it's fine to link directly to the video hosted on Youtube - as long as you're following all the other guidelines related to links.

But if the YouTube video is simply educating or entertaining your readers, you're safer embedding it on a page on your website and linking to that page.

Avoid Using Link Shorteners

Occasionally the URL for where you're sending traffic is quite lengthy, like the link to this blog post on Keap's website - https://keap.com/business-success-blog/sales/lead-magnet-landing-page-automation

Some people use services like Bitly to shorten the links so they don't take up so much space.

While that can be handy when posting links on social media posts, flyers, postcards, and other places, it can create problems with your emails hitting the inbox.

Spammers often use link shortening tools to mask links to malicious websites.

Because of this, Google, Microsoft, and Yahoo may **penalize you** for using a link shortener tool because they want to keep their users safe.

Layout

A **hotly debated topic** among email marketers revolves around the design and formatting of emails.

You'll understand and agree with some of my recommendations in this section. But you'll strongly object to others.

I guarantee you can find other email marketing experts who will present a different viewpoint and seemingly contradictory data.

The truth is, all marketing - no matter its form - is testing. What works in one market may not work in another. What moves one audience to action may not light a fire in another.

Your email style and design may create high engagement and conversion with *your* readers, but not with someone else's subscribers.

The advice I share is based on years of my personal research and experience.

So with that acknowledgement, let's begin.

A Look Through Your Inbox

Do an exercise with me.

Take 5 minutes to browse through the emails sitting in your inbox.

Look at three things about each email:

1. Who it's from
2. How it's designed
3. What its purpose is

When you're done, continue reading.

You most likely saw that emails sent from **big, well-known companies** like Macy's, Target, Chewy, Trade Coffee, and others **looked like marketing emails**. They are filled with color, different size text, several links, and lots of images.

If you're a Gmail or Google Workspace user, the bulk of those emails showed up in the Promotions tab. If you're a Microsoft user, you probably found lots of them in your junk folder.

On the other hand, emails from many of your **local shops and small businesses looked more personal**, like those from coworkers, friends, and family. Most used black letters on a white background, minimal links, and few, if any, images.

It's possible their emails also appeared in your junk, spam, or Promotions because those small business owners haven't read or applied what you've learned so far in this book.

But if they had, most of their emails would be seen in your inbox.

A Different Set Of Rules

It's also very likely that a decent number of ad-like emails from national stores and huge online brands showed up in your primary inbox.

Why?

Because of the volume of emails they send and their overall good email practices.

Let me illustrate.

Assume that your daily driving consists of only going to the post office from your house and back. There's one stop sign between your house and the post office.

You have a higher probability of getting pulled over and receiving a ticket for rolling through that stop sign because you're only making that one trip a day.

Whereas your neighbor, who spends all day criss-crossing your city going from store to store, can roll through more stop signs with no penalty simply because she's making more trips.

Similar logic applies to your sending of emails.

Because you're not sending thousands or millions of emails every month, **you're forced to abide by the stricter rules** set forth by Google, Microsoft, and Yahoo.

Once you ramp up the volume <u>and</u> prove you're not spamming people (i.e. doing everything you've learned in this book), you'll be able to get by with some things now and then.

Plain Emails Give Better Results

Which envelopes do you open first when sorting through your daily postal mail?

The ones that look personal, right?

Envelopes with images and words imprinted on them clearly identify themselves as marketing pieces and are often thrown to the side for perusing later. In some cases, you drop them directly into File 13.

The design of your email causes your recipients to respond in the same way.

A personal looking email, like we discussed earlier, often gets **opened and read immediately**.

An email filled with images, loads of color, and multiple fonts in different sizes communicates that it's a sales or marketing message and can be **put off until a later time** (which usually never comes) **or discarded into trash**.

Hubspot conducted multiple A/B tests comparing how text-only emails performed against highly designed emails.

> **"In every single A/B test, the simpler-designed (i.e. text-only) email won ... with statistical significance."**[18]

And from our exercise at the start of this section, you understand that the more your emails look like marketing, the less they will land in the inbox, instead showing up in junk, spam, or Promotions.

Focus on creating a beautiful, engaging website or landing page. Because 99% of the time, your call to action will direct your reader there.

That's where you really want to wow your reader.

So how should you design your emails?

Here are some rules of thumb to guide you:

- Left-justify your text.

- Open your email with words (preferably the recipient's name) not an image.

- Avoid using background colors.

- If using images, maintain a good text-to-image ratio, either 80% text and 20% images or 1 image per 3 full-length paragraphs.

- Keep your font usage clean and simple:
  - Use one body font at either 14- or 16-point type.

  - Use one headline font at either 20- or 24-point type.

  - No more than 2 colors.

A Word About Email Newsletters

I'm frequently asked my thoughts about sending email newsletters.

And you're probably questioning how you can make an email news-letter adhere to the design guidelines laid out above.

I'm personally not a fan of the typical email newsletter - the ones sent out once a week or once a month, link to several articles or blog posts, and look somewhat like an online newspaper.

A MailChimp study, reported by Backlinko, states that the open rate for email newsletters across all industries is 21.33%.[19]

Such a low open rate suggests that **most subscribers aren't interested in email newsletters**. While we don't know the specific reasons for this low engagement, I would surmise it's largely due to email news-letters looking like marketing content and because they bombard the reader with competing actions, creating indecision and confusion.

As I wrote earlier, people either immediately delete such emails or put off reading them, usually to never come back to them.

I would encourage you to invest your energy in creating offers and email communications that drive **high engagement and profitable conversions** with your list.

That being my official stance, I'm not saying you shouldn't send an email newsletter. A beautifully designed email newsletter might serve your audience and your business well. Test it.

Images

I strongly recommend that the majority of your emails - especially sales or other business critical ones - should not contain any images, except for your headshot or company logo in your email signature.

Sometimes, though, adding an image can illustrate a point you've made in your copy or allow your customer to see the product you're promoting.

Follow these guidelines to avoid common pitfalls that can keep your illustrated emails from being seen.

Keep Images Small

This recommendation relates to both **how your image appears** in your email and to **the file size of the image itself**.

Large images can cause your email to take longer to load, especially if it's being accessed on a cellular network, or be completely rejected by the mailbox provider. This is also why we warn against using one massive image as the only content of your email.

Appearance

- Balance the dimensions of your image so your email copy wraps neatly around it.

- Ensure images don't exceed the width of your overall email, which is usually 600 pixels.

File Size

- Use only JPG images 500 kilobytes or less in size.

- Resize large images using an online tool like TinyPNG.[20]

Add ALT Text

You may not be aware of a feature in most email marketing platforms that allows you to add ALT text to images you place in your emails.

ALT text is simply the **text that displays when an image fails to load**. It's suggested to keep your ALT text to 125 characters or less, including spaces.

It's important for two reasons.

First, it makes your email comply with accessibility standards. Some individuals with visual impairments rely on features like ALT text to consume content, and various states and countries are adopting laws to require it.

Second, some email clients do not show images by default. Microsoft's Outlook desktop software is the prominent one.

Including ALT text for all your images creates a better experience for your readers.

Limit The Quantity

It's worth repeating …

Plain emails generally outperform ones filled with images and beautifully designed.

When you do include images, keep it to 3 or less (including the one in your signature) and maintain the 80/20 text-to-image ratio we discussed above.

KEY TAKEAWAYS

1. Test variations of copy and design to see how mailbox providers deliver and how your list engages with different types of emails.

2. As a small business sending a lower volume of emails, you must abide by stricter rules than big corporations.

3. Business critical emails should more closely follow the guidelines in this chapter than non-essential emails.

4. Short, personal emails that look like one-to-one messages generally get better inbox placement and acted upon by your reader.

5. Take time to reword your calls-to-action so they don't look like marketing messages.

6. Limit the number of links to no more than 3 in each email - including ones in your email signature.

7. Check all links before inserting them in your email to see if the site you're pointing to appears on a blocklist.

8. Use social media links sparingly and only if they serve a specific purpose.

9. Make your website and landing pages beautiful; keep your emails plain and simple. Text-only emails often perform better than highly-designed emails.

10. When using images in an email, keep it to 3 or less and maintain the 80/20 text-to-image ratio.

Secret #4: Your Reputation Must Be Guarded

"It takes 20 years to build a reputation and five minutes to ruin it. If you think about that, you'll do things differently."
~ Warren Buffet

The ultimate success of your email marketing is determined by your reputation.

Google, Microsoft, and Yahoo heavily scrutinize many aspects of your online presence and behavior to determine what to do with the emails you send.

Of course, managing your engagement, setting up authentication, and transforming your content all factor into your overall reputation.

But it's **more than just your email behaviors**.

It also includes where you're emailing from, your list management, and anything related to your domain.

Two Types Of Reputation

Two types of reputation affect how the Big 3 mailbox providers judge you as an email marketer and what to do with your emails - **your sending IP reputation** and **your domain reputation**.

Sending IP Reputation

Email marketing platforms, like ActiveCampaign, Constant Contact, Keap, Mailchimp, and others, purchase blocks of IP addresses to assign to their servers used for sending their customers' emails.

Each email you send originates from one of those servers identified on the Internet by a unique IP address.

While most of the IP addresses serve as general delivery IPs, certain IP addresses are often reserved to only send emails to contacts who have double opted in to your list. Other IP addresses are used specifically for sending emails from new or low volume users.

No matter how your email marketing software divvies up their IP addresses, you and thousands of other email marketers will share the same IP addresses when sending emails.

Occasionally, this can cause problems getting your emails delivered.

Every once in a while, some user will violate the rules of good email practices (like the ones in this book) and cause one of the sending IP addresses to get blocked by Google, Microsoft, or Yahoo.

When this happens, everyone whose emails go out from the blocked IP address will either end up not getting delivered or going to junk/spam. These often show up as hard or soft bounces in your email marketing software.

The good news is that email marketing platforms hire experts, called postmasters, to constantly monitor and manage the reputation of all the IPs they use to send emails.

Fortunately, the postmasters work quickly to clear up these problems.

Although you have little control over your sending IP reputation, **managing your list by following the recommendations in this book can help get you placed on the IP addresses with the best reputation at your email marketing platform.**

Domain Reputation

Mailbox providers assign your domain (the part of your email address that appears after the @ sign) a score that indicates your risk as an email marketer.

It **works much the same way as your credit score**, both in how it's measured and how much control you have over it.

Consistently following good email marketing practices, such as monitoring engagement, setting up proper authentication, keeping your list clean, and sending useful content to your subscribers, increases your reputation.

You'll be **rewarded** with better inbox placement with each email you send.

On the other hand, a history of low engagement, improper or missing authentication, high bounce rates or spam complaints results in your reputation score plummeting.

You'll be **penalized** by the mailbox providers. They may choose to drop your emails in junk or spam. In severe cases, they may even refuse to accept and deliver <u>any</u> emails you send.

External Factors That Affect Your Reputation

Anything associated with your domain name reflects positively or negatively on your domain reputation.

This includes where your website is hosted.

In May of 2022, I discovered that any email I sent to a person who used a Microsoft-hosted email address (Microsoft 365, Hotmail.com, Live.com, or Outlook.com) went straight to the recipient's junk folder if it contained a link to my website - www.MasterPlan4Success.com.

Emails without a link to my website got delivered to the inbox.

Turns out, my web hosting provider's server was listed on a public blocklist.

This hosting provider also allowed users to set up POP3 email accounts to send and receive emails.

Somebody assigned to the same server where my website lived had been blasting out a bunch of unwanted emails, which caused the IP address of the server to get placed on the blocklist and create my email issues.

I contacted the web host to see if they would work with the blocklist to get their server's IP address removed. They refused, which sadly is the typical response of popular shared web hosting providers.

My only option was to move my website to a hosting provider who doesn't offer email hosting and takes security and reputation seriously.[21] As soon as I did that, the problems caused by the blocklist immediately disappeared.

How To Check Your Reputation

Google is the only mailbox provider who gives you insight as to how they view your domain reputation.

To see your score, you simply need to set up a Google Postmaster Tools account and complete the steps to verify your domain.[22]

You do need to have at least 500 to 1,000 Gmail and/or Google Workspace email addresses on your list <u>and</u> are emailing them consistently each month in order for any meaningful data to show in your Google Postmaster Tools dashboard.

You must also have DKIM configured for your email marketing platform.

Unfortunately, Microsoft and Yahoo don't reveal your domain reputation score as calculated by them.

However, reports we provide to subscribers of our Hit The Inbox™ Essentials and Active Marketer services can help you estimate how Microsoft and Yahoo view your domain reputation.

Now that you understand the two components that make up your reputation, let's explore how you can maintain a good one in the eyes of mailbox providers.

Keep Your List Clean

First, make sure you maintain **a clean list**.

List cleaning is an ongoing process. Much of it can be automated, while some of it will require manual effort.

Bot Submissions

The spammers, the hackers, and other nefarious people are out there in the world trying to sabotage as many people as they can.

I have no idea why, because a lot of times it doesn't actually make them any money. I guess they enjoy the thrill of making life difficult for hard-working, law abiding folks like you and I.

One tactic they use is **targeting forms on websites**.

Their malicious software fills in your webforms with somebody else's real email address or a fake email address so that it's now on your list. These are known as bot submissions, or spambots.

When you send an email to that address, it bounces (if it's a fake email address) or it gets marked as spam (if it belongs to someone who didn't legitimately opt in).

These actions drag down your reputation if they happen frequently or in high volume.

Preventing bot submissions on your webforms should be your first step to keeping them out of your database.

Enabling CAPTCHA on your webforms is one method built into most email marketing software.

This tool requires people to prove they're a human by selecting certain images of the same type from a grid, typing in characters displayed in a picture, or solving a math equation.

Unfortunately, many bot programs can successfully bypass CAPTCHA.

Not only that, a Stanford University study shows CAPTCHA can reduce your conversions by as much as 40 percent.[23]

The most effective tool I've seen that blocks the majority of spambots is **SpamKill**.[24]

It uses advanced techniques to prevent bots from detecting and filling in your webforms no matter whether you're using HTML code or a WordPress form plugin like GravityForms.

Inevitably, some bot submissions will make it through your best front-line defenses.

You'll want to **set up your email marketing software to alert you** when an email bounces or someone unsubscribes or reports an email as spam. This allows you to remove them from all future email communication, thus protecting your reputation.

Spam Traps

Have you ever experienced a moment of panic when you see a police cruiser tucked away in a hiding spot as you're cruising down the highway?

You quickly hit your brakes and look down at your speedometer to see if you were speeding.

If you weren't, you'll pass by their radar unscathed.

If you're guilty, you'll likely be forking over hundreds of dollars for a speeding ticket.

Police officers often set up speed traps in high traffic areas because they know they'll catch unaware drivers violating various traffic laws.

Similarly, mailbox providers, like AOL, Microsoft, Google, Spectrum, and Yahoo, set up their own **traps to catch email marketers not maintaining a clean list**.

These are called spam traps.

You'll encounter three types:

- Pristine spam traps

- Recycled spam traps

- Typo spam traps

Pristine Spam Traps

Just like the name sounds, pristine emails are squeaky clean. It's never been used to send email.

Mailbox providers create these addresses to identify **shady practices** of adding contacts to your list.

Pristine emails are embedded in websites. When spammers scrape websites for email addresses to sell or rent, these appear on the list.

When you buy one of these lists and send to these pristine email addresses, it tells the mailbox provider that you don't effectively manage your list and likely send out unsolicited email.

Pristine spam traps **cause the most damage** to your reputation. Most providers will completely reject all your emails if you're caught sending messages to these traps.

Recycled Spam Traps

Recycled spam traps get created from **valid email addresses** used by an individual or organization, but then stopped using it after a period of time.

Instead of shutting that email address down and you getting a bounce whenever you send an email to it, the mailbox providers keep it open and allow it to accept emails.

Continuing to email these addresses tells mailbox providers that you don't maintain or have a good relationship with your list.

Typo Spam Traps

Typo spam traps are **misspelled email addresses**, often the domain name - like "gamil.com" instead of "gmail.com".

Of course, mistakes can happen when someone enters their information on a web form, so not all typos are spam traps.

Keeping your list free from spam traps can be as simple as:

- Not buying or renting email lists.

- Regularly running all contacts through a list cleaning utility.[25]

- Using email validation on your opt in forms to catch typos.

- Closely watching engagement and removing subscribers who haven't recently engaged with your emails.

Manage Your Engagement

Managing your engagement is vital to the success of your email marketing.

Failure to do so can eventually **damage your reputation beyond repair**.

Reread Secret #1 to make sure you have a firm grasp on how to measure engagement and what actions to take to increase it.

A Guaranteed Way To Damage Your Reputation

The package looked like any other normally arriving in the United States from overseas.

Various homemade food items and gifts filled the box from top to bottom. A normal care package sent to family members.

But the U.S. Customs and Border Protection agents know what looks legit on the surface can be a cover for illegal contraband not visible at first glance.

As they examined the box with their x-ray machine, tell-tale signs indicated that some of the usually hollow items were stuffed with foreign objects.

A physical inspection revealed nearly $30,000 worth of cocaine almost made it into the country.

The rest of the *To Catch A Smuggler* episode followed Homeland Security Investigations agents as they hunted down and arrested the intended recipient of the package.

Some email marketers operate in similar underhanded ways, trying to game the system to force their emails into their target's inboxes.

They **employ tricks** to fool the machine learning algorithms that scan their emails.

They **take advantage of loopholes** allowing their seemingly innocuous activities to go unnoticed.

While these may be successful for a time, eventually Google, Microsoft, and Yahoo identify these schemes and bring down the hammer.

The screenshot below shows a real warning Google sent to an email marketer. This individual used a third-party "warm-up" software to send unsolicited emails to people who had not opted in for their messages.

They got by with it for a while.

Until they didn't.

Google issued an ultimatum - stop the bad behavior or we'll cut off your ability to use our API.

You can be sure Google documented this, will continue to closely monitor this person's activities, and slashed their domain reputation score significantly.

Don't try to game the mailbox providers. It's not worth inflicting damage on your reputation.

Visit **HitTheInboxBook.com/audit** to request your Hit The Inbox™ audit and explore other valuable resources. Use promo code **BOOK20** to receive $20 off.

[Time Sensitive] Compliance with Gmail API Services User Data Policy

Hi,

We found during a compliance audit that your project ID ~~~~~ ~~~~ is in violation of the **Gmail API Services User Data Policy**:

- Applications that use multiple accounts to abuse Google policies, bypass Gmail account limitations, **circumvent filters and spam**, or otherwise subvert restrictions are prohibited from accessing Gmail API scopes.

To maintain access to the Gmail API, you must disable the email warming feature by **February 13, 2023**. If you are unable to remedy these violations, your access to the Gmail API will be revoked.

To ensure user messages are not flagged as SPAM, we recommend your users instead set up SPF, DKIM, and DMARC email standards for Gmail by following these instructions.

For more information, refer to the following resources:

- OAuth Application Verification FAQ
- Google APIs Terms of Service
- Gmail API Services User Data Policy
- Google API Services User Data Policy

Thank you for your patience. If you have any other questions, please reply directly to this email. Note that any new emails sent to api-oauth-dev-verification@google.com won't go to our team.

A warning from Google

KEY TAKEAWAYS

1. The ultimate success of your email marketing is determined by your reputation.

2. Your reputation is made up of your sending IP reputation and your domain reputation.

3. Your domain reputation works much like your credit score. You have the most control over managing your domain reputation.

4. Keeping your list clean and managing your engagement are the top two ways to maintain a good domain reputation.

5. Never buy or rent email lists. These often contain pristine spam traps, which can severely damage your domain reputation.

6. Attempting to circumvent the rules and best practices established by mailbox providers will only hurt you in the long run.

What To Do Next

Congratulations on finishing this book. You now know and understand the foundational requirements to get more of your emails delivered and seen to get more sales.

As I mentioned in my introduction, you likely picked up this book because you either:

- **Know you have problems** with people seeing your emails, causing you to lose sales, and you want to fix them ASAP ... or

- **Want to proactively prevent issues** and generate as much interest and revenue as possible from your email list.

In the words of Bruce Lee, "Knowing is not enough. We must **APPLY**."

If you want your emails to avoid the spam folder ...

If you want your prospects and customers to read your emails ...

If you want to get a better return from your email marketing ...

You cannot afford to be like the 200 small business owners who *did nothing* when I showed them critical issues rendering their email marketing ineffective.

Instead, you need to **request your Hit The Inbox™ audit** at HitTheInboxBook.com.

You'll receive a real-time snapshot of your Email Health Score.

You'll see if your list is filled with liabilities who are damaging your reputation every time you send an email or if it's full of assets who actively engage with most of your communications.

You'll know if your authentication is properly configured or if you're "emailing without a license."

Finally, you'll get a prioritized action list outlining what issues, if any, you need to correct.

The choice is yours.

Will you be satisfied with simply reading this book cover to cover or will you seize the unfair advantage available to you by taking action and requesting your Hit The Inbox™ audit today?

Visit **HitTheInboxBook.com** to request your Hit The Inbox™ audit and explore other valuable resources.

Use promo code **BOOK20** to receive $20 off.

Citations

[1] https://www.moengage.com/blog/ensure-email-delivery-gmail-inbox/

[2] https://help.activecampaign.com/hc/en-us/articles/115001622504-The-hype-and-truth-about-Gmail-tabs

[3] https://help.activecampaign.com/hc/en-us/articles/115001622504-The-hype-and-truth-about-Gmail-tabs

[4] https://help.activecampaign.com/hc/en-us/articles/115001622504-The-hype-and-truth-about-Gmail-tabs

[5] https://dataprot.net/statistics/spam-statistics/

[6] https://www.statista.com/statistics/456500/daily-number-of-e-mails-worldwide/

[7] https://thebettyrocker.com/youre-almost-done/

[8] https://thebettyrocker.com/thank-you-bgp-guide/

[9] https://www.youtube.com/watch?v=eq6adAKY7xM

[10] https://senders.yahooinc.com/best-practices/

[11] https://www.campaignmonitor.com/resources/guides/email-marketing-new-rules/

[12] Sending domain means the domain name from which you send emails. It's what appears after the @ sign in your email address.

[13] https://www.sendx.io/help/list-of-spam-trigger-words

[14] https://blog.hubspot.com/blog/tabid/6307/bid/30684/the-ultimate-list-of-email-spam-trigger-words.aspx

[15] https://www.activecampaign.com/blog/spam-words

[16] https://blogiestools.com/email-spam-trigger-words-checker-tool/

[17] https://mxtoolbox.com/blacklists.aspx

[18] https://blog.hubspot.com/marketing/plain-text-vs-html-emails-data

[19] https://backlinko.com/email-marketing-stats

[20] https://tinypng.com/

[21] Flywheel is my recommended web host - https://share.getf.ly/s09f7d

[22] https://www.gmail.com/postmaster/

[23] https://web.stanford.edu/~jurafsky/burszstein_2010_captcha.pdf

[24] https://spamkill.co/

[25] https://www.klean13.com/

Scott A. Hartley

Serial entrepreneur and founder of MasterPlan4Success, Scott Hartley understands the challenges small business owners face.

He knows what it's like to wear all the hats in a business. Like you, he discovered there were aspects to running a business few entrepreneurs talk about - taxes, payroll, insurance, hiring (and firing!) employees, and marketing, to name a few.

Scott built his first company into a multi six-figure business from scratch. Through much trial and error, hard work, and hours of study and implementation, he discovered what worked to grow his business, as well as what didn't.

In 2017, Scott decided to take his knowledge and experience and help other small business owners shortcut their path to success by helping them with marketing strategies, systems and business automation, and getting their emails delivered.

He has helped attorneys, IT consultants, financial advisors, psychologists, bakers, community organizations, and many others make more money and get and keep more customers without feeling overwhelmed and overworked.

Scott has been privileged to share the virtual stage with experts like Grant Cardone, Loral Langemeier, Kim Walsh Phillips, David Milton, Dr. Anthony Criniti IV, and others. He has been mentored by Craig Ballantyne, Brendon Burchard, Frank Kern, Dan Kennedy, Tony Robbins, Robin Robins, and other business experts throughout the years.

In his free time, Scott enjoys being outside in nature, reading, traveling, playing piano and keyboard, and spending time with friends. Scott sang at the famed Carnegie Hall in New York City in May 2022 as part of a national choir led by world renowned composer/conductor Pepper Choplin.